CREATIVE LIVES

Northamptonshire
County Council
Libraries and Information Service

D0766245

JEREMY WALLIS

LIBRARY

80 001 929 122

Scl

H **www.heinemann.co.uk/library**
Visit our website to find out more information about **Heinemann Library** books.

To order:
☎ Phone 44 (0) 1865 888066
▤ Send a fax to 44 (0) 1865 314091
▯ Visit the Heinemann Bookshop at www.heinemann.co.uk/library to browse our catalogue and order online.

First published in Great Britain by Heinemann Library, Halley Court, Jordan Hill, Oxford OX2 8EJ, a division of Reed Educational and Professional Publishing Ltd. Heinemann is a registered trademark of Reed Educational & Professional Publishing Ltd.

OXFORD MELBOURNE AUCKLAND JOHANNESBURG BLANTYRE
GABORONE IBADAN PORTSMOUTH NH (USA) CHICAGO

© Reed Educational and Professional Publishing Ltd 2001
The moral right of the proprietor has been asserted.

All rights reserved. No part of this publication may be reproduced, stored in a retrieval system, or transmitted in any form or by any means, electronic, mechanical, photocopying, recording, or otherwise without either the prior written permission of the Publishers or a licence permitting restricted copying in the United Kingdom issued by the Copyright Licensing Agency Ltd, 90 Tottenham Court Road, London W1P 0LP.

Designed by Tinstar Design (www.tinstar.co.uk)
Originated by Ambassador Litho Ltd.
Printed and bound in Hong Kong/China

ISBN 0 431 13985 7   (hardback)   ISBN 0 431 13992 X   (paperback)
06 05 04 03 02 01   06 05 04 03 02
10 9 8 7 6 5 4 3 2 1   10 9 8 7 6 5 4 3 2 1

British Library Cataloguing in Publication Data
Wallis, Jeremy
    Coco Chanel. – (Creative Lives)
    1.Chanel, Coco, 1883-1971 – Juvenile literature
    2.Women designers – France – Biography – Juvenile literature
    3.Fashion designers – France – Biography – Juvenile Literature
    I.Title
    746.9'2'092

Acknowledgements
The Publishers would like to thank the following for permission to reproduce photographs: AKG: pp10, 36, 53; Bettmann/Corbis: p26; Bibliotheque Nationale: p13; Corbis: p41; F. Kollar/Ministére de la Culture, Paris: p40; Harlingue-Viollet: p8; House of Chanel, France: pp24, 32, 47, 35; Hulton Getty: pp6, 29, 31; Hutin, Compiégne: p11; Kobal/John Miehle: p34; Lebrecht Collection: p17; Musée des Arts Décoratifs, Paris: p23; Robert Doisneau/Rapho/Network: p48; Roger Schall: p21; Roger Viollet: pp37, 44; Rue des Archives: pp12, 15, 49; Sotheby's London/Cecil Beaton: p4; Sygma: p16, Horst p54; Topham: pp30, 33, 51; © Vogue, Condé Nast Publications Inc: pp5, 19, 25, P. Horst p38, John Rawlings p39; Wladimir Rehbinder courtesy of Vogue, Paris: p28.

Cover photograph reproduced with permission of Corbis.

Our thanks to Suzanne Lussier for her comments in the preparation of this book.

Every effort has been made to contact copyright holders of any material reproduced in this book. Any omissions will be rectified in subsequent printings if notice is given to the Publisher.

Disclaimer
All the Internet addresses (URLs) given in this book were valid at the time of going to press. However, due to the dynamic nature of the Internet, some addresses may have changed, or sites may have ceased to exist since publication. While the author and Publisher regret any inconvenience this may cause readers, no responsibility for any such changes can be accepted by either the author or the Publisher.

Any words appearing in the text in bold, **like this**, are explained in the Glossary.

Contents

Introduction

> *'From this century, in France, three names will remain: De Gaulle, Picasso and Chanel.'*
> André Malraux, writer and French Minister of Culture, 1971

The Irish philosopher and intellectual George Bernard Shaw was asked to name the most important women of the 20th century. 'Marie Curie and Coco Chanel!', he replied without hesitation.

You may only know the name Chanel from the label on a perfume bottle. But the story of Gabrielle 'Coco' Chanel is of interest to anyone curious about fashion and art in the 20th century, in the European **avant-garde**, theatre, ballet and cinema, and for students of 20th-century history in its triumphs and tragedies.

For many, Chanel epitomizes the **Jazz Age** – a glamorous world of beautiful people living in luxury while **depression**, war and hunger swept the globe.

But it would be wrong to dismiss Chanel simply as a dressmaker who made herself rich and famous by dressing wealthy clients. In fact she was one of the most remarkable women of the century, living at a time of great artistic, political and social change. Her life paralleled the growing assertion of **women's rights** and the

Gabrielle 'Coco' Chanel strikes a pose in evening dress, between two Nubian statues – photographed by Cecil Beaton.

development of the **mass market** for women's fashion. If the changes in women's status between 1918 and the 1970s constituted a **revolution**, then perhaps it can be said that Chanel designed the uniforms for it!

Chanel began designing clothes at a time when women's bodies were constrained by whalebone **stays**, complicated trimmings and accessories – when they had to wear impractical costumes that even lacked pockets. Of the elaborate hats, Chanel once asked, 'how can a brain work under those things?'

Function versus form

Chanel changed all that. She let function determine form, so that the purpose of a costume influenced its design. Her outfits were comfortable, sensible, stylish and, for many, affordable. She was also never afraid to criticize designers who failed to recognize the real shape of women's bodies: 'Someone tells you: "The shoulder is on the back." I've never seen women with shoulders on their backs.'

For years Chanel's influence on women's fashion was total. She made trousers acceptable, popularized short hair, and revolutionized swim and sportswear. As a fashion innovator, anything she did was noticed. One possibly exaggerated story tells of Chanel standing on the deck of a yacht. Feeling cold, she borrowed a man's jacket, but because the sleeves were too long she draped it over her shoulders – and accidentally started a fashion copied by thousands! Coco is even credited with making suntans fashionable.

Illustration of Chanel's *Garçonne*-style daywear in woollen printed jersey, from British *Vogue*, 1928.

Chanel in 1929, in a straw cloche hat. Her career spanned the great events of the 20th century.

Chanel was also an innovative businesswoman. Her simple garments could be reproduced easily by seamstresses or department stores. The fashion magazine *Vogue* compared her most famous design – the 'little black dress' – to the Model-T Ford motorcar. She was flattered by imitations of her designs. She launched Chanel No.5, the first perfume to bear a designer's name, and recognized that perfume, not **haute couture**, was the secret of success. Her expensive clothes sold the myth of Chanel style, but Chanel No.5 was the essence of the myth that any woman could afford.

Chanel was on intimate terms with the leading lights of the avant-garde. Like a magpie attracted to bright and shiny objects, she borrowed ideas from wherever she saw fit: from Egyptian artefacts, Russian peasant and gypsy styles, men's wear, British sporting fashion, working-class garments and oriental dress.

Chanel's story mirrors the events of the 20th century; from World War I, the Jazz Age, the Wall Street Crash and the **Great Depression** to World War II, the **'affluent society'** of the 1950s, and the alternative culture of the 1960s. When she died, in 1971, she was the figurehead of a **multinational** fashion empire – quite an achievement for a child born in poverty and brought up in an orphanage.

The beginnings

Who was Coco Chanel? Coco Chanel told lies about herself and her past. Even when she was old, and had endured many decades in the limelight, she told lies. Coco Chanel created more than clothes, hats and jewellery; she invented herself.

Born Gabrielle Chanel, she was the second child of market traders. Her father, Albert Chanel, was a 27-year-old trader in wine, buttons, hats and kitchen aprons. Her mother was Jeanne Devolle. Albert met Jeanne in 1881 when she was seventeen years old and living with her family in the village of Courpière in the Auvergne region of France. In January 1882 he left, leaving Jeanne pregnant. Jeanne discovered Albert's whereabouts and, alone and heavily pregnant, she travelled the 200 kilometres to Aubenas where Albert had a room in a tavern. The couple's first daughter, Julia, was born there in September 1882. Three months later, now living in Saumur on the River Loire, Jeanne fell pregnant again.

Gabrielle was born in the Saumur **hospice** on 19 August 1883. Hospice staff gave her the name Gabrielle, and she would always resent it. When two **illiterate** hospice employees registered her birth at the town hall, they took no documents to confirm the status of parents or child. The deputy mayor improvised, misspelling her last name 'Chasnel' on the birth certificate.

The mistake was never rectified; to correct it might have revealed her hospice birth. And though her parents married after she was born, Gabrielle always feared people might learn of her **illegitimacy**. In later life, she claimed her father had been a wealthy horse trader. She even paid her brothers to keep quiet, and denied their existence. To some, Gabrielle explained the manner of her birth as an accident that befell her mother while travelling to her husband. To others she claimed she had been born in a train carriage!

After Gabrielle, Jeanne gave birth in quick succession to Alphonse, Antoinette and Lucien. A third son died in infancy. Although the children often stayed with Jeanne's family in Courpière, life on the

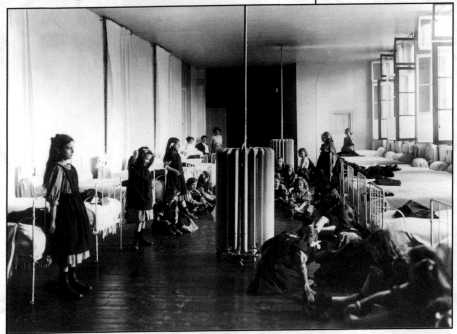

An orphanage in France at the end of the 19th century. Though Chanel found life hard at Aubazine, she also took strength from the discipline and orderliness.

road, poverty and constant pregnancies destroyed Jeanne's health, and she fell ill. One winter morning in 1895 Jeanne was found dead in her room. She was only 32 years old. Albert Chanel, who was away at the time, abandoned his children and disappeared.

Members of Jeanne's family were happy to have the children at holiday time, but could not take them in permanently. Instead, Gabrielle, Julia and Antoinette spent six years in an orphanage run by sisters of the Congregation of the Sacred Heart of Mary at Aubazine. Alphonse and the infant Lucien were 'placed' in a farming household to provide unpaid child labour.

> " Chanel found strength in suffering. *'I've been ungrateful towards the odious aunts [but] I owe them everything. A child in revolt becomes a person with armour and strength… It's the mean and nasty aunts who create winners, and give them **inferiority complexes**… Under nastiness looms strength.'* "

In adulthood Chanel sliced years off her age and dropped Julia, Alphonse and Lucien from her life story. She told people she was six when her mother died and rarely talked of the orphanage, describing the nuns as 'aunts'.

Although life was hard, Gabrielle took pleasure in the cleanliness, simplicity and orderliness at Aubazine. She described herself as fierce, pretty and restless; she also knew she was different: 'I was a pest, a thief, someone who listens at doors. Today, like back then, arrogance is in everything I do.' She found comfort in solitude, spending time in cemeteries talking to the dead. To save embarrassment about her family background, Gabrielle told classmates her father was seeking his fortune in America and would come for her when he was rich. In reality she never saw him again.

During the holidays with her grandparents, Gabrielle grew close to Adrienne, an aunt her age. They often passed themselves off as sisters. Adrienne's older sister, Louise, rescued Gabrielle's brothers from the farms and put them into apprenticeships with market traders. The orphanage taught Gabrielle to sew but Louise showed her how to do it with imagination.

After six years at the orphanage, Julia and Gabrielle attended boarding school in Moulins, a small **garrison town**. Antoinette joined them a year later. Reliant on charity to pay for lodging and food, the girls also worked to pay their school fees. To cater for the military, Moulins had many restaurants, cafés and tailors' shops. By the age of 20, Gabrielle had a reputation as a skilled dressmaker. She also worked with Adrienne in a tailor's shop to supplement her income. Soon young cavalry officers were coming into the shop as much to see 'The Three Graces' – as Gabrielle, Adrienne and the sixteen-year-old Antoinette were nicknamed – as they were to have their uniforms altered.

The most fashionable entertainment of the day was the *café concert*. There were many in Moulins, well attended by young officers and their families. Though working as both a dressmaker and tailor's assistant, Gabrielle had serious ambitions to become a singer and entertainer.

The girls started to accept invitations to concerts at a large, popular café called La Rotonde. In the days before electric amplification, singers needed to take regular breaks to rest their voices. Young women – called *poseuses* – sat on stage and filled in during these pauses. Audiences pelted *poseuses* with cherry stones if their performances were not up to scratch!

Chanel pictured around 1909. Though trained as a dressmaker, Gabrielle Chanel had ambitions to be a singer.

Bolder than the others, Gabrielle took a turn at singing. Though her voice was not strong, she carried the day with a song about a young woman looking for her dog. 'I've lost my poor Coco,' she sang, 'Coco my lovable dog…' Chanel soon became a regular. Audiences knew her as *La Petite Coco* ('Little Coco'), and the name stuck. Though Chanel eventually accepted that she only had limited abilities as a singer, and that a career as a *café concert* performer was not going to happen, her love of the stage and of being in the public eye would often emerge in later life.

Moving on

When she was 21 years old, Chanel became involved with Etienne Balsan, an army officer three years her senior. Etienne was the wayward son of a rich textiles family. His passion was horses: once out of the army he wanted to breed them.

Some biographers believe that Chanel became pregnant by Etienne early in their relationship. Soon after, Julia, Chanel's sister, also fell pregnant by a fairground worker who refused to marry her. Having no intention of bringing up an **illegitimate** child, as her mother had and her sister was about to, it has been said that Chanel underwent an **abortion**. This may have affected her **fertility** in later life.

In 1905 Etienne left the army and asked Chanel to visit his château, Royallieu. The appeal of a singing career was waning for Coco and she lacked the **dowry** needed to attract a respectable young man. So she accepted Etienne's invitation. She was to stay for years.

The château at Royallieu, where Coco was registered in the 1906 census as 'Gabrielle Chanel, *sans profession*' (without occupation).

Life at Royallieu

Like many rich young men, Etienne Balsan was indulged by his family. He surrounded himself with famous and wealthy people. His acquaintances – aristocrats, sportsmen, racehorse owners – liked to bring women to Royallieu who were not their wives. Many of these female guests were themselves unconventional and independent – women like Gabrielle Dorziat, a well-known actress of the time who became a close friend of Chanel's.

Chanel became what was termed an *'irrégulière'*: a woman who lived as a wealthy man's wife but whom, because she was neither respectable nor aristocratic enough, he could not marry. Chanel spent her years at Royallieu learning to ride well, attending horse races and enjoying the luxuries of the **belle époque**.

Many wealthy men of this time kept mistresses as symbols of their wealth. The most famous mistresses were the 'diamond crunchers' – so-called because they received valuable love tokens such as diamonds. But a new feminine ideal had emerged – the **Claudines**. Inspired by the **semi-autobiographical** novels of Colette, *Claudines* were young, quick-witted and defiant: freer in style and ready to break social restrictions. This 'new woman' was celebrated in plays, paintings and songs. The campaign for women's **suffrage** was intense at this time – women were soon allowed to become

A busy tavern in France during the *belle époque*, around 1900, showing fashions worn by both men and women of the time.

This fashion photograph by Seeberger Frères, from around 1909, shows the fussy hats and clothes of the period.

lawyers, and shop-girls were even permitted to sit if there were no customers to serve! Like a typical *Claudine*, Chanel set herself apart from others, by the way she dressed and the way she lived.

Chanel's first fashions

In contrast to the flamboyant, frilly glamour favoured by others, Chanel preferred plain clothes. She marked herself out by wearing simple costumes and small hats. She later confessed that when she first arrived at Royallieu, her wardrobe consisted of two tailored suits and a jacket, adding that the origins of her costumes were the tailored costumes she had worn as a teenager.

When riding, a skill that earned her the admiration of Etienne and his friends, Chanel was every inch the modern sportswoman. She sat astride the horse rather than riding side-saddle, and she raided Etienne's wardrobe for clothes and ideas. She wore tailor-made outfits – jodhpurs (riding breeches) cut from a stable-groom's pattern, a riding-jacket and a shirt with collar and tie. This was very **radical** at a time when most women rode in 'safety skirts' over breeches.

Chanel, however, was still very insecure. Intimidated by the beauty and status of the women guests at the château, and undermined by her lowly social origins, Chanel compensated with a sarcastic manner and wit. Yet all the time she carefully observed the behaviour and **etiquette** of the social **elite** she mixed with.

Etienne and Coco got on well but she later confessed she did not love him. Etienne's family despaired of him, and one account says that Etienne's brother actually asked Chanel to marry Etienne and make him 'respectable'. Chanel turned the offer down.

Life at Royallieu was easy. Removed from the outside world – a world of great change, bursting with new ideas – the pattern of Chanel's life was straightforward. Friends and acquaintances recalled how she would often emerge from her room only at lunchtime, unless a horse ride was promised, in which case she would be dressed and eager to get on at the break of dawn.

Chanel grew bored. To keep herself occupied, she bought plain straw hats at the Galeries Lafayette store in Paris and decorated and trimmed them herself. These were much more attractive than the fussy plumed hats of the time and women friends asked where she bought them. Emilienne d'Alençon, an infamous 'diamond cruncher' and one of Etienne's former lovers, brought Chanel to wider public attention by wearing one at the horse races. Emboldened, and perhaps with one eye on her future security, Coco asked Etienne to finance a hat shop in Paris.

France and the *belle époque*

The *belle époque* – the period before World War I – was a prosperous time and also a time of exciting change, pregnant with new ideas.

Industrialization brought large-scale **urbanization** and with it new social problems. Working people campaigned to improve their lives. Leisure – picnics, fêtes, boating trips – became important as people sought refuge from city life, encouraged by the development of the railways. French governments became **nationalistic**, anti-**socialist** and anti-German, fearful of socialist **revolution** and German aggression. In the arts, France was recognized as the world centre of **Modernism**.

New influences
and directions

In 1908, while Etienne pondered Chanel's business idea, they travelled to Pau, to hunt in the Pyrénées. On the trails below the snow-capped mountains, Chanel met the love of her life: Arthur Capel, an Englishman everyone called 'Boy'.

Boy Capel had financial interests in coal and shipping, and was an excellent horseman. He and Coco spent hours in each other's company. When Coco learned one evening that he was leaving for Paris, she wrote a note to Etienne: 'I am leaving with Boy. Forgive me, but I love him.'

She left without even a suitcase. Coco later made herself out to be an awkward eighteen-year-old. In fact she was 25. Coco moved into Boy's apartment, on avenue Gabriel. Although many people in polite society frowned upon their relationship because they were not married, Boy introduced Coco to a new circle of painters, writers and actors where their unconventional relationship went unnoticed.

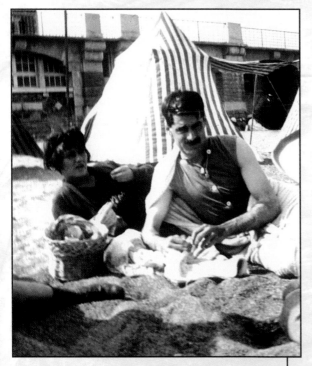

Arthur 'Boy' Capel and Coco enjoy a picnic on the beach.

The beginnings of the Chanel empire

Chanel remained on good terms with Etienne. Though he refused to finance her hat shop, he agreed to let her use his apartment on boulevard Malesherbes as a base. The business opened in 1909.

Soon, many of Chanel's female acquaintances were buying her chic, stylish hats. They, in turn, introduced their friends. Although Chanel worked hard, she was soon forced to employ a professional **milliner** and, later, two assistants. Recognizing both her abilities and her ambition, Boy loaned Chanel money to open a boutique. Chanel Modes opened at 21 rue Cambon in 1910.

Chanel the brand

Chanel recognized the importance of the relationship between the worlds of theatre and fashion. In the days before television, film and radio, stage actresses and dancers could establish fashion trends that were then featured in newspapers and fashion magazines.

In 1910, actress Lucienne Roger wore a Chanel hat on the cover of *Comoedia Illustrée*. There were enthusiastic reviews, and illustrations of other actresses wearing Chanel hats. Soon Gabrielle Dorziat was buying all her hats from Chanel Modes; she wore Chanel hats on stage and was pictured in one in *Journal des Modes* in 1912.

Chanel's name became as well known as the stars she worked for. But, unlike them, she liked to preserve an air of mystery and often hid in the backroom of the shop, out of sight. 'A client seen is a client lost,' she once said.

By 1913, Chanel's business was financially secure. When Julia, her elder sister, died suddenly Coco was able to assume financial responsibility for the education of Julia's son, André Palasse. She also employed her younger sister Antoinette, who no longer had Julia to rely on.

Gabrielle Dorziat, famous actress and friend of Coco Chanel, wearing a Chanel hat in 1912.

The fashion houses of Paris

In Paris in the first decades of the 20th century, there were several established *maisons de couture* – such as Worth, Doucet and Paquin – and a publishing industry that thrived on reporting what society figures and actresses were wearing. Fashion magazines carried news of the latest styles: rigid corsets that pinched the waist so tightly they made eating difficult and affected breathing; layers of skirts; trimmings of lace, beads, sequins and feathers. Then, as now, popular culture had a major influence on fashion. For example, in 1908 Paul Poiret introduced a new, looser style inspired by Eastern fashion and Serge Diaghilev's modern ballet company, the Ballets Russes.

Moving in unfamiliar circles

Chanel's interest in the arts grew. Seeing the brilliant modern dancer Isadora Duncan perform inspired Chanel to take dance lessons. Her teacher, a former performer called Caryathis, was blunt – Coco had no talent. However, she invited Chanel to the opening night of *Le Sacre du Printemps (The Rite of Spring)* by Igor Stravinsky, performed by the Ballets Russes.

Photo of the Ballets Russes production of *Le Sacre du Printemps* (The Rite of Spring) by Igor Stravinsky. Chanel secretly funded a revival of this controversial ballet, and also had a relationship with Stravinsky.

A previous Stravinsky ballet – *The Firebird* – had been a sensation and Parisians looked forward to the new piece. It was premiered on 13 May 1913. Despite its title, *The Rite of Spring* is not full of lambs and spring flowers; it is a powerful representation in music and dance of a **pagan fertility rite**. At its climax a maiden is sacrificed to the gods in return for making the soil fertile. Chanel was at the premiere and watched in amazement as the audience rioted! The dancers were booed, and Stravinsky took refuge backstage while his opponents and supporters tussled in the aisles.

This marked the start of Chanel's association with the **avant-garde** in general and Diaghilev and Igor Stravinsky in particular.

Deauville

In the summer of 1913, Boy Capel took a suite at the grand Hotel Normandy in Deauville. Every summer, wealthy visitors filled this chic coastal resort. They entertained themselves sailing, gambling and watching horse races. Capel realized it was a perfect market for Chanel: she left Antoinette in charge of Chanel Modes in Paris and opened a shop on the most stylish street in Deauville.

Until 1913, the sea was for looking at or sailing on – only a hardy few (including Chanel) actually swam in it. The rich sneered at suntans as the mark of a peasant lifestyle spent working outside in all weathers. Instead, the affluent classes protected their fair complexions with **parasols** and hats. However, sport and an active outdoor lifestyle were becoming both popular and fashionable. Coco conquered Deauville by introducing a fashion whose time had come – sportswear.

Chanel liked the sweaters worn by English sailors. She picked one up at a polo match because she was cold. It was too big and she cut the front open so it would not have to be pulled over the head, added ribbons and a knotted belt. 'People asked me, "Where did you find that dress?" I said, "If you like it I'll sell it to you." I sold ten like that... My fortune is built on that old jersey I put on because I was cold.'

In doing so, she wrote the rules that marked her career as a designer: function dictated form. By 1917, the loose, comfortable *tricot marinière* was immensely popular around the world.

Illustration of a model wearing Chanel's *tricot marinière* in emerald green silk jersey fabric, from American *Vogue*, 1 June 1917.

Chanel also had a champion in the cartoonist Sem, who compared her simple, straightforward designs to the over-fussy fashions of the time. He also showed her as a society personality – a 'face' who was changing the social standing of designers. Before Chanel, fashion designers were considered little more than 'tradespeople' who might be snubbed by their clients in any social situation. Soon, however, they were the people to be seen with. 'I started a fashion,' she said, ' – **couturiers** as stars.'

Fame and fortune during World War I

During World War I, away from the fighting, there were winners as well as losers. Boy Capel's interests in coal and shipping and his contacts in the British and French governments made him wealthy and influential. Coco also emerged a winner. Because of rationing and conflict, discretion replaced opulence. Fashion was turned upside down: as women became involved in war-work, clothing had to suit their active lifestyle.

With the declaration of war Deauville initially emptied of people. Boy returned to England. As the German army advanced on Paris, panic gripped the city. Theatres, shops and galleries were closed, the French government moved to Bordeaux, resources were diverted to prepare the city's defences. Deauville now filled with wealthy women, sent from the capital by their husbands. Shrewdly, Chanel kept her shop open – it was the only one left in town. Antoinette and Adrienne left the Paris boutique and joined the third 'Grace' once more.

Modesty prevails

There was also a demand for sober yet smart fashion. Excessive displays were considered bad taste when young men were dying at the front. By the end of 1914, Paris was no longer threatened by the Germans. As the military situation stabilized, shops reopened and business resumed.

The government allowed theatres to reopen, but banned jewellery and evening dress. Chanel's style was perfect: her smart, functional look suited the mood and practicalities. Women were encouraged to slim down to use less fabric. Coco sold the new slimness: 'with the war's connivance, all my clients lost weight, to "become skinny like Coco"'. Coco cut her hair short – making a 'bob' – blaming it, in the Chanel legend, on an accident with a faulty water heater. The cut was stylish and practical. Women loved it.

In 1915, Chanel opened a boutique in Biarritz – a resort close to Spain. Biarritz attracted Spanish visitors, where elegance was still in vogue. Spanish and American women soon formed a large part of Chanel's clientele. *Harper's Bazaar* magazine announced, 'the woman who hasn't at least one Chanel is hopelessly out of the running in fashion'. By 1916, 300 staff were employed by Chanel in Paris, Deauville and Biarritz.

The Chanel method

In Biarritz, Chanel's **maison de couture** sold tailor-made outfits to wealthy Parisians living out the war in luxurious exile. Sixty people were employed in the shop and workrooms. Despite the war, there was still a trade in luxury fabrics: Chanel established relationships with industrialists and dyers in France, England and Scotland.

Chanel and a group of mannequins in the 1930s. Many of Chanel's favourite models and mannequins bore a remarkable resemblance to Coco herself.

Chanel liked people to think she was a lady of leisure. But she actually worked very hard – sometimes for up to seven hours on a single outfit. She did not sketch outfits but created garments by draping material around young women – **mannequins** – paid to stand very still for a very long time. She crouched before them, tugging, stretching, folding and stitching, her scissors dangling from a long ribbon round her neck. First a muslin toile (blueprint) was made. When it was perfect –

21

The jersey revolution

Knitted jersey material was introduced around 1880. Made of finely knitted wool, jersey clung to the body but was elastic. It was used to make men's underwear and sportswear. In 1916, a fabric manufacturer called Jean Rodier offered Chanel a huge stock of jersey. The natural stretch made it difficult to sew, but Chanel solved the problem by making simple, supple shapes. Many people were shocked that Chanel was using it for women's clothes, but with these garments she turned knitted jersey into high fashion. In 1917, *Vogue* called the House of Chanel 'the Jersey House'. *Les Elégances Parisiennes* featured Chanel's jersey designs in March 1917.

and up to 30 might be created before Chanel thought it was – the toile was used to make the final garment in the selected fabric.

And woe-betide the mannequin who complained or moved while posing – they might be jabbed by Chanel's pins! Nor were they well rewarded: when asked about their poor wages Chanel retorted, 'They're beautiful. Let them take lovers!'

Waking up famous

By the end of the war in November 1918, 1.5 million Frenchmen had been killed and the treasury emptied: the country was in ruins. Old beliefs and ways of life were gone too. There were irreversible changes in culture and the way women saw their place in the world.

Paris quickly recovered in the post-war years and soon dominated art, culture, fashion and design. The American Gertrude Stein said Paris was 'where the 20th century is'. Almost everything of importance written or painted in the first years of peace was done there. It was a city where you could do or get anything; where the sounds of dancing and jazz carried on all night long.

Acclaimed alongside artist Pablo Picasso and writer and film-maker Jean Cocteau, everything was going right for Coco. '1919 was the year I woke up famous' she said. But tragedy loomed.

Costumes de Jersey from the magazine *Les Elégances Parisiennes*, 1917. Chanel turned a workaday fabric used by bathers, racing-cyclists and fishermen into high fashion.

End of an affair

While Chanel and Boy had seen great success, a distance had grown between them. In 1918 Boy had suddenly married Lady Diana Wyndham. But despite his marriage he still wanted Coco in his life. In December 1919 Boy spent several days with Chanel in Paris, before leaving for the south of France to spend Christmas with his wife. On the journey his car overturned and burst into flames. Boy Capel died in the fire.

Coco was profoundly distressed and her emotions were further injured when she was prevented from attending the funeral. Instead, a friend, Léon de Laborde, drove her to the scene of the accident, where she stood alone and still on the scorched and blackened road. Afterwards, to block out her grief, Chanel immersed herself in her work. But she later pledged she would put the whole world in mourning for Boy.

A few months later, Coco's sister Antoinette died. After the death of their elder sister Julia, Chanel had been very protective of Antoinette. During the war, Antoinette married a Canadian airman and returned to Canada with him. But before long she ran away with a young Argentinean to Buenos Aires. She died on the other side of the Atlantic from Chanel, a victim of the influenza epidemic that swept the globe after the war. Once more, Coco parcelled up her sorrow and devoted her energies to the Chanel business.

'The Roaring Twenties'

" *'Women no longer exist; all that's left are the boys created by Chanel!'* "
Marquis Boni de Castellane

Chanel style typified the 'new woman' – a woman who could work and live by her own code. It was a statement by the wearer about herself. Chanel helped popularize the new feminine shape, free from clutter and corsets. To some, however, the 'new woman' looked more like a boy.

The launch of Chanel No.5

By 1920, Chanel was ready to diversify her business. In that year she had an affair with the famous Russian Grand Duke Dimitri. Thanks to Dimitri, she met Ernest Beaux, who had been employed at the Russian Tsar's court. In 1921 she launched Chanel No.5. It was the first perfume to bear a **couturier's** name, and Chanel commissioned Ernest Beaux to make it. No.5 was the fifth formula of nine that he created.

Traditionally, perfumes were blended from expensive natural ingredients to emulate flowers and other natural scents. Chanel No.5 was the first perfume blended to smell uniquely of itself rather than imitate nature. Chanel designed the simple **modernist** bottle herself.

Coco established No.5 as the essence of the Chanel ideal. Women who might never afford a Chanel original outfit could buy part of the Chanel mystique in a bottle.

To maximize sales, Chanel agreed to let Les Parfums Bourjois – France's largest perfume and make-up company – produce and market Chanel No.5. A new company was set

A design classic, Chanel's minimalist bottle for Chanel No.5 would become almost as world famous as the Coca Cola bottle.

up in 1924: Les Parfums Chanel. Because Les Parfums Bourjois committed themselves to all the production, marketing and distribution costs, Coco agreed to take a share of the profits. Such **franchising** was very new in the 1920s.

Coco's relationship with Pierre and Paul Wertheimer, owners of Les Parfums Bourjois, soon became thorny. Seeing what a success Chanel No.5 was, Chanel convinced herself that she had given the rights away too cheaply and began legal proceedings to get a bigger share. By 1928, the Wertheimers employed a lawyer solely to deal with her lawsuits.

Coco and the Russians

Chanel's relationship with Grand Duke Dimitri inspired many of her creations. Aristocratic **exiles** came to Paris in the aftermath of the 1917 **Russian Revolution**. Exiled women who once considered embroidery a leisure activity now had to earn a living. They found it embroidering the large plain blocks of fabric in Chanel's designs. Clearly influenced by her many Russian acquaintances and friends, Chanel introduced a version of the peasant *roubachka* – a long belted blouse – made in luxurious silk, in 1922. Her embroidered shift dresses became very popular. The House of Chanel also employed several Russian artists disillusioned with art in Soviet Russia.

Chanel's *roubachka* and embroidered dress. Coco's interest in Russia and the Russians influenced both her professional work and her personal life.

> " 'Women think of all colours except the absence of colour... Black has it all. White too. It is the perfect harmony,' said Chanel. "

The little black dress

By the mid-1920s, fashion was dominated by the *Garçonne* look, named after a popular novel by Victor Margueritte. *Garçonnes* – or 'Flappers' in America – shared Chanel's slender, almost **androgynous** figure, cropped hair and short hemlines. In 1926, Chanel launched her 'little black dress'. Copied around the world, it became the 'uniform' of the *Garçonne*. The fashion designer Paul Poiret described it as '*pauvreté de luxe*' (luxurious poverty). 'Simplicity doesn't mean poverty,' Chanel retorted.

The simplicity of the 'little black dress' had a worldwide appeal. This Chanel original 1960s 'little black dress' was sold at auction in December 1978 for £1,500 (US$3,000).

While men had worn black for years, women only wore it as a sign of mourning. Chanel herself believed black was elegant and would never go out of fashion. She hated the eccentricity of bright colours – Poiret's 'barbaric reds, greens and electric blues' – and ornate designs. 'That can't last,' she said of women in their elaborate dresses. 'I'm going to dress them simply, and in black.'

You can have any colour...

The spread of Chanel style owed itself to a variety of factors. Her straightforward designs lent themselves to imitations: they overcame size problems, required little fabric and were easy to copy using **mass production** techniques. **Synthetic** fibres enabled manufacturers to make garments at a fraction of the cost. Women who could not afford a Chanel original could easily buy a **rayon** copy.

More expensive copies came from dress shops that copied direct from the Paris shows and copy houses that bought originals; less expensive copies came from manufacturers who worked from illustrations and photographs, and were therefore less exact. This range of copies flattered designers like Chanel, who knew that no one would mistake a copy for an original.

In 1926, American *Vogue* printed a picture of Chanel's little black dress. 'Here is a Ford signed Chanel', they announced. 'The frock the world will wear.' Equating it to the Ford car, *Vogue* predicted it would become a worldwide uniform for women. As Henry Ford famously said of his first automobile: 'You can have any colour, as long as it's black.'

" In 1927, Winston Churchill, later to become prime minister of Britain, " wrote to his wife after meeting Coco: *'She hunted vigorously all day, motored to Paris after dinner, and is today engaged in passing and improving dresses on endless streams of **mannequins**. Altogether almost 200 models have to be settled in almost three weeks. Some have to be altered ten times. She does it with her own fingers.'*

Chanel and the avant-garde

The first three decades of the 20th century were a time of incredible artistic development. Technological innovation, science, **mass production**, war and political change inspired artists. Film and photography became increasingly important.

A scene from *Antigone*: Genica Atanasiou, on the right, plays Sophocles' defiant heroine Antigone in a cape of brown wool – one of the costumes Chanel designed for the play.

Chanel's association with the artistic world first began when she and Boy lived together in Paris. She had also been deeply affected by the riotous scenes at the premiere of *The Rite of Spring* (see page 17). Chanel's connections were strengthened by Misia Sert, a woman she met in 1917. Misia became a lifelong friend and Chanel later acknowledged Misia's role as her teacher in cultural and artistic subjects.

Misia introduced Coco to Jean Cocteau, an influential

Make it new!

Modernism – the name given to **radical** artistic experiments – provoked enthusiasm and violent outrage; for example, the riots at the premiere of *The Rite of Spring* and fights at another ballet called *Parade*. The latter had music composed on typewriters by Erik Satie and outrageous costumes by the Spanish artist Pablo Picasso. **Avant-garde** is the name given to artists and writers whose ideas are the most modern of their time.

writer and film-maker. In 1922, Cocteau asked Chanel to design costumes for his adaptation of the ancient Greek writer Sophocles' tragedy *Antigone*. Pablo Picasso, who came to dominate 20th-century art, designed the sets, actors' masks and shields.

Chanel dressed the actors in Greek-style costumes of coarse, undyed wool. Genica Atanasiou played Antigone with her hair cropped short, face whitened and eyes rimmed in thick black make-up. Chanel dressed her in a full-length, hand-knitted coat with Greek vase motifs in maroon and black. However, feeling her contribution was being overlooked, Chanel seized a loose strand and unravelled the coat! Too late to fix the damage, Genica had to go on stage in one of Chanel's own coats. Another character wore a gold headband encrusted with jewels, Chanel's first effort at jewellery.

A scene from *Le Train Bleu*. The ballet was inspired by the then current vogue for sportswear – a fashion Chanel herself had done much to popularize.

In the reviews, Coco stole the headlines: 'Chanel becomes Greek' proclaimed one. French *Vogue* featured Chanel's costumes in February 1923.

In 1924, continuing her association with Serge Diaghilev's Ballets Russes, Chanel designed costumes for *Le Train Bleu* (The Blue Train) composed by Darius Milhaud with words by Cocteau. Inspired by the fashion for sport, the ballet mixed **satire**, song, mime and acrobatics. The name was taken from a luxury train that ran from Paris to the Côte d'Azur. Dispensing with traditional tutus and tights, Chanel's costumes were startling. The female lead wore a tennis outfit and the male lead a golf outfit of fair-isle jumper and 'plus-fours', based on an outfit worn by the British Prince of Wales. One dancer wore a pink bathing suit – very daring for the time – and a skullcap that set a fashion trend.

By lending her talents to the avant-garde, Chanel's name became associated with Modernism. She was also generous in her financial support. She secretly funded a revival of Stravinsky's *The Rite of Spring* (and had an affair with the composer). She also supported Cocteau, often paying his hotel bills and helping him battle drug addiction.

Chanel designed for ballets and plays throughout the 1920s. She was also very shrewd and a keen promoter of her business. In *Orphée*, Jean Cocteau's 1926 version of *Orpheus and Eurydice*, Chanel simply had the actresses dress in her latest fashions!

All that glistens...

The Chanel business empire took another new direction when Coco turned her love of extravagant costume jewellery into high fashion.

'Costume jewellery' is fake jewellery, designed to look real. Chanel's radical idea was to design the jewellery to coordinate with her fashions or 'costumes'.

Costume jewellery meant women could 'have fortunes that cost nothing'. She believed 'jewels... give an air of elegance or decoration'. There was nothing more foolish than women dripping in real jewels: too much money, she said, killed luxury.

Coco pictured in 1928, wearing strings of fake pearls and about to get into her chauffeur-driven Rolls Royce.

As always, Chanel herself broke every convention about wearing jewellery. Traditionally women wore discreet pieces in the daytime and more showy pieces at night. Contrarily, Chanel draped herself in strings of jewellery during the day, even when sailing or on the beach, and in the evening often wore no jewellery at all. The fashion designer Christian Dior later said, 'With a black sweater and ten rows of pearls she **revolutionized** the world of fashion.'

Coco in love (again)

There were several men in Chanel's life after Boy, but any who tried to force her to choose between him and her work would lose!

Coco Chanel with the Duke of Westminster at the Grand National horse race in England in 1925.

Her most famous relationship was with the Duke of Westminster, Britain's wealthiest man. The Duke kept two yachts, had a residence in London, Eaton Hall in Cheshire, a Scottish estate, a hunting lodge near Biarritz, a suite in Paris and a château in Deauville. The Duke was related to Winston Churchill, the future British prime minister.

They met in Monte Carlo at Christmas 1923 and gossip magazines were soon predicting they would marry, but Chanel had no intention of sharing him with a succession of mistresses. Once, when he tried to please her with expensive emeralds, Chanel let the

31

emeralds slip from her hand into the ocean in a gesture of defiance. When the relationship ended, Chanel claimed, 'There have been several Duchesses of Westminster. There is only one Chanel!'

Chanel's next relationship was with Pierre Reverdy, a poverty-stricken poet. Reverdy believed happiness was an illusion. To chase pleasure, he told Chanel, was to chase the wind. His outlook sat uncomfortably with the giddy '**Jazz Age**' and his poetry enjoyed little success. When he died, Chanel tried to rescue his reputation from obscurity. It was Reverdy who inspired her belief in an afterlife and the idea that nothing ever disappeared.

Chanel relaxes at La Pausa, her residence near Menton on the French Riviera, with her dog Gigot.

Good times and bad

The House of Chanel continued to expand throughout the 1920s as it supplied the seemingly insatiable demand for luxury goods in Europe and the USA. Then, in October 1929, the Wall Street Stock Market in New York crashed. This event changed everything as the resulting economic **depression** dramatically hit the luxury trade.

For a while the rich continued to amuse themselves, unconcerned by the effects that economic collapse had on their fellow countrymen and women.

The collapse of the world economy had huge repercussions in France. Here, unemployed men queue for soup and bread in the Parisian district of Montmartre.

The Great Depression

In the years after World War I the USA became the world's most powerful nation. Between 1913 and 1929, the economy grew by 70 per cent. The **New York Stock Exchange** on Wall Street became the world's leading stock market. Between 1927 and 1929, share prices rose spectacularly. People used savings, borrowed and even mortgaged homes to buy more. Then, on 24 October 1929, prices dropped suddenly. People lost businesses and homes; companies closed; millions lost their jobs. Because of the importance of the USA to the world economy, the Wall Street Crash made economic problems around the world much worse. Those dependent on exporting to the USA were hardest hit.

As late as 1930, extravagant balls were being held in Paris. However, the demand for **haute couture** dried up. Paul Poiret closed his fashion house and his creditors seized everything. Within months of the Wall Street Crash, 10,000 French fashion workers had been sacked.

Gloria Swanson in the 1931 film *Tonight or Never*, wearing a Chanel-designed outfit.

Chanel managed to survive. Wealthy customers from India and South America offset the loss of US customers and the richest of her European customers stayed loyal. In addition, by 1931 it was considered bad taste to look wealthy; rich women bought the plain dresses, furless coats and sweaters that were the core of the Chanel line. Chanel was also invited to London to promote cotton as a fashion fabric.

Coco goes to Hollywood

Sam Goldwyn, the powerful Hollywood film producer, realized that the cinema had to attract more women filmgoers to survive the economic crisis. He believed women wanted movies with big stars wearing the latest clothes. It was risky – fashions could change quickly, so outfits might have been out of date by the time a film was released!

Goldwyn had first met Chanel in 1929. In 1931, she signed a contract to design outfits exclusively for his stars. Chanel, then the most famous **couturier** in the world, travelled to Hollywood, California, in a blaze of publicity. Though confident of her own abilities, her time in America was not a success. Chanel's designs turned out to be too modest for most film stars. As *New Yorker* magazine noted on her return to France in 1932: 'She made a lady look like a lady. Hollywood wants a lady to look like two ladies.'

Although Chanel was forced to cut her clothes prices in half at the height of the depression in 1932, the $2 million she earned in Hollywood enabled her to keep the company afloat. The House of Chanel continued to expand and employed over 4000 workers by 1935.

In 1932, Chanel created a range of diamond-encrusted precious jewellery. This typical comet necklace was one of several shown at an exhibition in that same year called Bijoux de Diamants.

Back to jewellery

The economic depression also offered other opportunities. In 1932, in an effort to boost sales, the International Diamond Guild commissioned Chanel to create a range of diamond jewellery. Previously she had popularized false jewellery in a time of affluence, but she now believed diamonds were an investment during economic depression.

Working with jewellery designer Paul Iribe, who became her lover, Chanel presented designs based on three shapes: knots, feathers and stars. Many pieces – extravagantly encrusted with diamonds – could be used as brooches or hair ornaments, necklaces or tiaras.

Chanel took inspiration from Hindu artefacts, Christian symbols, the medieval world. Later there were brooches based on sea anemones, necklaces of oak leaves and acorns. By 1939, brilliant bib-necklaces were sewn directly on to dresses.

Love and politics

" Of her relationship with Paul Iribe, Chanel later said, 'He drained me, ruined my health.' "

Paul Iribe had spent the 1920s in Hollywood designing sets for the film-maker Cecil B. De Mille. Returning to France, he built a successful business but went bankrupt. Iribe began designing jewellery for the famous jewellery maker Cartier and for the House of Chanel. His experiences of the economic **depression** had made him very **right-wing** and **anti-Semitic**.

At the time he and Coco became lovers, in 1931, Chanel's relationship with the Wertheimers was at a new low. Chanel No.5 had become the world's best-selling perfume, and the Wertheimers wanted to market other beauty products under Chanel's name. She opposed this and they wanted to remove her as president of Les Parfums Chanel. She gave Iribe **power of attorney** to act for her, but he chaired a board meeting so incompetently that the members voted him out. Les Parfums Chanel began granting manufacturing rights for Chanel products to other companies controlled by the Wertheimers.

As a **nationalist** and **elitist**, Paul Iribe condemned **republican** government and wanted to see a strong ruler. He persuaded Chanel to finance his political magazine *Le Témoin*. It was one of many nationalistic, anti-German magazines then being published in France.

Chanel pictured in 1931, the year she and Paul Iribe became lovers. He moved her political views to the right.

In 1934 there was an unsuccessful rebellion by right-wing militants. It provoked communists and **socialists** to form a **'Popular Front'**. Many people feared that **Bolshevism** was just around the corner. Influenced by Iribe, Coco moved from political indifference to a belief that socialism threatened France.

In 1934, Iribe and Chanel announced they would marry. Not everyone was happy: the novelist Colette wrote, 'Iribe is marrying Chanel. Aren't you horrified – for Chanel?'

However, Iribe suffered a heart attack playing tennis with Coco at La Pausa, her residence in the south of France. He died in hospital in Menton, aged 52 years. Once again, Chanel took refuge from her sorrow in work.

Chanel and the Arts

Despite her experiences in Hollywood, Chanel had not finished with theatre, movies or with the **avant-garde**. In 1934, she designed costumes for Jean Cocteau's *La Machine Infernale*. Cocteau was by now very influential but he still relied on Chanel's support for his hotel

Chanel's mummy-style costumes for *Oedipe Roi*, by Jean Cocteau, were fiercely criticized in the press for their 'indecency'.

bills and **detoxification** cures. When Cocteau revived *Oedipe Roi*, Chanel dressed the dancers in revealing Egyptian mummy-style wrappings, which were criticized in the press as indecent.

Despite her political views, Chanel remained on good terms with many socialist artists. The film-maker Jean Renoir asked Chanel to create the wardrobe for his film *La Marseillaise* and only conflicting schedules prevented Chanel working on his anti-war masterpiece *La Grand Illusion*. A year later, Chanel designed costumes for *La Règle du Jeu (Rules of the Game)*, Renoir's **satire** about a house-party

Chanel and Schiaparelli

Chanel's greatest rival was Elsa Schiaparelli, also famous for designs she created with Salvador Dali. In contrast to Chanel, Schiaparelli used vivid, even startling, colours, notably Tyrian purple, renamed 'shocking pink'. Her collections were built around colourful themes – the circus, music, and butterflies – and influences from African art. Here a model wears an outfit with butterflies on the jacket and hat.

Chanel and Schiaparelli could not stand each other. Chanel called Schiaparelli 'that Italian who makes clothes'. Schiaparelli referred to Chanel as a 'dreary little bourgeois'. But each kept a close eye on the other's work. In dividing the same pool of clients, they were creating 'schools' of fashion: Chanel was increasingly seen as a 'safe' designer, while Schiaparelli was considered more adventurous.

gathering for a hunt where the masters and servants turn upon and shoot each other! At the premiere, the furious audience tried to set fire to Renoir's chair!

Chanel also formed a friendship with the Spanish artist Salvador Dali, a leading **surrealist**. Dali composed *Bacchanale* for the Ballets Russes and asked Chanel to design the costumes. Later he said, 'Chanel... created some of the most luxurious costumes... real ermine, real jewels.'

Strike at the House of Chanel

In April 1936, the people of France elected Socialist leader Léon Blum and his Popular Front into government. Blum promised to introduce holidays, family support, unemployment benefit and a 40-hour working week.

In 1938, Chanel's love of gypsy style influenced her work. Full skirts of multicoloured taffeta were worn with embroidered blouses and short bolero jackets. Suits were decorated with bright braid and embroidery.

The French Constitution prevented Blum from taking office until June. French workers feared their hopes might be dashed before he took power and a wave of strikes and American-style 'sit-ins' began. Unrest spread to the notoriously badly paid textiles industry. On 6 June 1936, as Chanel arrived at rue Cambon, she was confronted by a **picket line** of striking saleswomen and seamstresses who refused to let her into the House of Chanel. Seething at their behaviour, Chanel retreated to her suite at the Hotel Ritz.

The wave of strikes was soon settled in return for wage increases, union recognition, a 40-hour working week and two weeks holiday each year. Chanel responded to the settlement by dismissing many of her staff, but this simply hardened their determination.

According to her lawyer, René de Chambrun, Chanel was **paternalistic**. She had little empathy with her poorly paid staff, despite her own humble origins. She wilfully misunderstood the phrase '**sit-down strike**', claiming workers were sitting on her dresses. However, commercial pressure to produce an autumn collection, and de Chambrun's careful advice, forced Chanel to settle.

Coco pictured in her suite in the Ritz, in 1937. In the late 1930s, Chanel's eveningwear became more elaborate.

Surviving occupation in World War II

Outside the world of *haute couture*, war clouds gathered. Style and fashion seemed frivolous, highly inappropriate to the national mood. On 2 September 1939, Hitler's army invaded Poland. Britain and France declared war on Germany. Explaining that it was no time for fashion, Coco closed the House of Chanel.

The war reaches Paris

Surprisingly, after the declaration of war, a sort of peace broke out. Soldiers at the front exchanged more words than bullets; from their positions, German troops cheered football matches played between French infantrymen. German **propaganda** blamed England for the war. Many Frenchmen agreed, seeing little reason to die for Poland.

A **blackout** was implemented in Paris, but cinemas and theatres reopened. Fashion designers presented collections. For the rich, there were inconveniences – butlers and chauffeurs were **conscripted** and petrol was rationed – but normality returned. Chanel took a suite at the Ritz. Jean Cocteau also stayed there, in a room Chanel paid for.

Hostilities started in earnest in April 1940. Hitler's generals developed 'Blitzkrieg' – lightning-war. Helped by **Allied** indecision, poor

German troops stage a victory parade in the shadow of the Arc de Triomphe in Paris.

equipment and inadequate leadership, the Germans swept through Western Europe. On 4 June, Paris was bombed and *l'exode* – the escape of the city's civilian population – began. Millions took to the road, carrying what they could in buses, horse-drawn carriages and cars, or on cycles and handcarts.

France governed from Vichy

Chanel packed a few belongings and her collection of precious jewellery and she and a friend set off south, away from the German forces. However, en route they heard the news that the Italian **Fascist** leader Mussolini had launched air raids on the Riviera in support of his Nazi ally. Changing direction, Chanel and her companion made for Biarritz, near the Spanish frontier.

Meanwhile, French military leaders declared Paris an 'open city' and pulled back. Within six weeks the Germans were almost at Bordeaux and the French signed a humiliating armistice (peace treaty): the Germans occupied northern France while an 'independent' French government ran the south from the town of Vichy.

In August, as the situation stabilized, Chanel decided to return to Paris. Stopping for a break in a small village, she saw a child begging. Her normal reserve and haughtiness cracked and she gave the child several coins. Immediately the child's mother appeared and took the money off him: 'At least we shall eat tonight,' the woman said. For Chanel, it was a horrifying example of the state that France had fallen into.

French resistance

Following World War II, the French promoted an image of heroic **resistance** to the Nazi invaders. In fact, some people were willing **collaborators** in some of the Nazi's most horrific crimes. The US ambassador at the time wrote, 'French leaders... have accepted... becoming a province of Nazi Germany.' When the Germans put **anti-Semitic** laws into place in northern France, the Vichy government went even further in its anti-Semitism.

Arriving in Paris, Chanel discovered that the Germans had taken over the Hotel Ritz, including her suite. One story claims she told the manager to inform German high command that Chanel had arrived! In another, a German officer noticed her name on her luggage and said: 'If we're talking about the Mademoiselle Chanel of fashion and perfume fame, she can stay.' Whatever the truth, Chanel got a room.

Selling out

Though she had closed her *haute couture* salons in 1939, there was a boutique on rue Cambon selling Chanel perfumes and accessories. Coco visited it soon after her arrival in Paris. It was full of German soldiers buying Chanel No.5. When stocks ran out, they bought empty display bottles – anything to prove they had been in Paris.

To secure the release of her nephew, André Palasse, then a prisoner of war, Chanel approached Hans Gunther von Dincklage, a former member of the German embassy staff in Paris and rumoured to work for German military intelligence.

'My friends call me Spatz,' he said. 'German for sparrow.' Despite their age difference – Spatz was twelve years younger – they became lovers. They lived together at the Ritz until 1944 when, as Allied forces were about to liberate Paris, Spatz fled back to Germany.

Under the occupation an eccentric normality returned. The Germans encouraged theatres, cinemas and newspapers to open, and helped many of Chanel's **avant-garde** acquaintances. For the wealthy **elite** – despite shortages for everyone else – luxuries were in plentiful supply.

Chanel had her pre-war fortune to support her and was also sustained by the sales of Chanel No.5 throughout occupied Europe. Like many wealthy people, she and Spatz held parties for the Franco-German elite, who were not going to let war interfere with the social niceties. Meanwhile, gossip magazines claimed Chanel and Cocteau were to marry. This story emerged in 1943, at a time of growing organized resistance to the invaders and high-profile collaborators, and deflected attention from the fact that Chanel actually had a German lover who was a member of the occupying forces.

German soldiers at the theatre in Paris. Germans stationed in France were able to enjoy the best of French culture.

War and the Wertheimers

It was at this time that the Vichy government's Commission for Jewish Affairs handed many Jewish businesses to non-Jews. The Wertheimers, who were Jews, had gone into hiding before escaping to the USA, leaving the company in the hands of a cousin, Raymond Bollack. Although Chanel showed no interest in design or fashion at this time, she saw an opportunity to end the difficult partnership. However, Bollack found a non-Jewish industrialist, Félix Amiot, to front the company and a German officer to certify everything was in order. Chanel was foiled once again. No.5 continued to be sold by the French company and, unknown to Chanel, by the Wertheimers' smaller US company.

Chanel was involved in attempts to save individual Jews from Nazi concentration camps. The Jewish poet and painter Max Jacob, who was associated with some of the greatest figures of the French avant-garde, was a friend of Chanel's. Already seriously ill, Jacob was arrested and taken to a transit camp at Drancy near Paris. The next stage of his journey would be to the death camps in Poland. Chanel helped in the desperate efforts made by his friends to save him. The authorities were eventually persuaded that he was too ill to travel and he was released. Unfortunately Jacob died soon after.

An end to hostilities

By 1943 America's involvement in the war in Europe and in the Pacific was in full swing. The German army was struggling on the **Eastern Front** and facing defeat at Stalingrad in the Soviet Union and in North Africa. For many Germans the question of defeat was not 'if' but 'when' and 'how'.

Like many people, Chanel believed that the Russians would eventually defeat Germany. Hitler still believed he could defeat both the Russians and the **Allies**, but many senior Nazis thought the best option was for Germany to make a quick peace in the West, or even form an anti-communist alliance with the Allies against the Soviet Union.

There is one fascinating wartime story, the complete truth of which will never be known. During her relationship with the Duke of Westminster, Chanel had got to know Winston Churchill, who was by now the prime minister of Britain. It was suggested that Chanel could ask Churchill to listen to secret proposals from within the German high command, advocating that Germany and the Allies should arrange a peace treaty. Chanel would to go to Spain, meet the British ambassador and request a meeting with Churchill.

Through Spatz, elements of the German high command agreed and gave her the go-ahead for what became known as Operation 'Modellhut'. Chanel asked that Vera Bate, an English friend married to an Italian, be her travelling companion. Vera was brought to Paris where Chanel explained they were reopening the House of Chanel in Madrid. However, Vera saw it as an opportunity to escape occupied Europe. The involvement of German security agents in whisking her from Rome to Paris made her believe that Chanel was a German spy.

As soon as they arrived in Madrid both made their way separately to the British embassy. As Chanel met the ambassador to request a meeting with Churchill, and pass on the news that elements within the German high command wanted to negotiate, Vera was denouncing Chanel.

Operation 'Modellhut' was doomed to fail. Churchill was at that time too ill to see Chanel, and in any case firmly against compromise with Hitler's Germany. Instead Chanel travelled back to France, her friendship with Vera in ruins.

Liberation and fear

After the defeat of the Germans and the liberation of France, there were scores to settle: **collaborators** were jailed, property seized, women with German lovers had their heads shaved. There were many summary executions. Though Spatz had fled back to Germany, Chanel realized her high profile and close association with a German officer like Spatz would make her a prime target.

The journalist Malcolm Muggeridge has said that, using her wits, Chanel placed a notice outside her perfume boutique announcing free Chanel No.5 for American soldiers. They queued in huge numbers, preventing **Free French** police from arresting her. Using this breathing space, she sought help from her contacts. Finally taken in for questioning by the Free French authorities, she was released after three hours and no charges were ever brought. It is likely that Chanel knew more about the level and degree of collaboration than many in power wanted revealed in open court.

Exile and fortune

The end of the war also meant the return of the Wertheimers. They had been making and selling their own Chanel No.5 in the USA, and Les Parfums Chanel was now a subsidiary of an American company, Chanel Inc. Coco realized they had made millions: her **royalties**, deposited in a Swiss bank, amounted to a few thousand dollars. She had been had – yet again! More than the stain of her relationship with a German, it was the strain of the ensuing legal battle that caused her to move to Lausanne, in Switzerland.

There was another reason: Spatz had been captured in Germany by the Americans and held as a prisoner of war. He was soon released but a return to France was out of the question. In Switzerland, he and Chanel were able to live together without attracting hostility or comment.

American soldiers queue in front of the Chanel boutique at 31 rue Cambon in 1945 to buy No.5 perfume for wives and girlfriends.

In 1947 Chanel and Pierre Wertheimer came to an agreement to compensate Chanel for the lost earnings. Satisfactory to both sides, the agreement renewed their business relationship and placed it on a much more respectful and convivial footing.

Though now very rich, Chanel's name was fading from fashion consciousness – only women with long memories remembered her style; younger women knew her only as the name on a perfume bottle. Coco confessed she was simply a bored old woman, drifting back and forth between Switzerland and France. Life had changed beyond recognition: she and Spatz parted, and many friends and former lovers died in the post-war years.

The return of Coco Chanel!

In 1954, at the age of 71, Coco Chanel announced her comeback. The editor of *Vogue*, Bettina Ballard, said 'she [returned] to escape boredom and to keep young'. A woman called Marie-Hélène de Rothschild claimed credit for inspiring Chanel's return. Seeing Marie-Hélène in an expensive ball gown, Chanel exclaimed 'what a horror!' and immediately improvised a substitute from a taffeta curtain! After the ball, Marie-Hélène reported that everyone had asked who the designer was.

But apart from the desire to design again, Chanel also had financial motives. In spite of Marilyn Monroe's famous remark, 'the only thing I wear in bed is Chanel No.5', perfume sales were not very strong. So she moved back into the Paris Ritz, the boutique and workrooms at 31 rue Cambon were renovated and former members of staff were recruited. Coco began working on a brand new collection.

Chanel photographed by Robert Doisneau on the mirrored staircase of 31 rue Cambon, on the eve of her comeback in 1954.

Chanel and the New Look

Chanel still believed in the virtues of a flattering look that was easy to wear and did not date quickly. But she now thought that styles that were unsuitable for most people were not fashion but fancy dress. In particular, she thought the elaborate 'New Look', unveiled by Christian Dior in 1947, was not the way forward. Sweeping aside austere wartime fashion, the New Look returned to luxury with long full skirts, rustling with layers of petticoats, tight-fitting bodices and jackets with tiny waists, created with tight corsets that emphasized the '**hourglass**' figure. One writer said these corsets pulled the

Dior's 'New Look', with a characteristically exaggerated waistline.

waist in so much it was a choice between not eating or suffering acute indigestion. Chanel commented that the pulled-in waistline was 'an exaggeration even on a wasp'.

Chanel's 1954 collection was a response to the New Look she so despised. But it was also a response to the increasingly fashion-conscious **mass market** that demanded stylish but less expensive designs in large quantities. It was to **revolutionize** fashion. By using newly available **synthetic** textiles and modern production techniques, companies could make **ready-to-wear** outfits quickly and cheaply, reaching a massive audience.

Pierre Wertheimer recognized Chanel's comeback would rekindle perfume sales. He also realized that as owner of Chanel Couture,

Coco could **franchise** her name – cheapening the prestige of Les Parfums Chanel. Pierre decided he had to invest in the Chanel revival: Les Parfums Chanel paid part of the cost of the collection from their publicity budget.

In interviews Chanel restated her philosophy, 'elegance... means freedom to move freely'. Of the Spanish designer Balenciaga she said, 'Didn't his customers look like armchairs?' The British photographer Cecil Beaton was allowed to picture her at work – unheard of given the secrecy surrounding fashion launches.

The collection was shown to the **elite** of the fashion world on 5 February 1954. The models appeared quietly, without the razzamatazz of a Dior parade. The collection was greeted in silence, and damned in subsequent reviews. Chanel was, commentators said, 'a prisoner of the age she influenced so strongly'. Others were more harsh: Le Combat ran a headline, 'In the sticks with 1930 Coco Chanel.' The British Daily Express reported, 'A Fiasco – Audience Gasped!' In an interview with France-Soir, Coco explained: 'Once I helped liberate women, I'll do it again.'

'I want to go on... and win,' she told Pierre Wertheimer. 'You're right,' he said, pledging the support of Les Parfums Chanel. Three weeks later, the American magazine Life carried rave reviews. 'Like her best of the thirties... elegant dash... easy-fitting suits that are refreshing after the "poured-on" look.' The March issue of French Vogue followed, with a Chanel-suited model on the cover. Karl Lagerfeld, then a young apprentice designer, said the look was 'more intoxicating than any current fashion'. Coco was back.

Coco and the men

In the inter-war years, women – Chanel, Schiaparelli, Vionnet, Madame Grès – dominated fashion. The top names were now men: Mainbocher, Dior, Jacques Fath – inventor of the guêpière or waspie corset – Givenchy, Pierre Cardin. Schiaparelli admitted defeat and closed her house in 1950.

" 'Dressing women is not a man's job. They dress them badly because they scorn them.' Chanel in 1953 "

The men were different. They worked on paper rather than moulding their creations on models. Designs were more daring, possibly because they did not have to wear them; practicality was secondary to effect. Outfits grew bolder, more outrageous: skirts in the shape of pumpkins and trumpets, coats like tents, 'sheath dresses' as tight as skin. Chanel was on the side of women: clothes were to be comfortable. She did not believe that designers such as Dior had women's interests at heart.

Chanel set to work on her next collection. Soon buyers and the press 'rediscovered' Chanel: classic chic was back. She used jersey, tweeds, satin, chiffons, velvets, synthetic fibres, in her favourite colours – red, black, beige, white and blue. Women famous for their elegance wore her designs: Grace Kelly, Lauren Bacall, Ingrid Bergman, Elizabeth Taylor, Rita Hayworth, Marlene Dietrich. As it does today, celebrity endorsement brought further recognition.

This year's model: the 1959 variation on the classic Chanel Suit.

Though she designed a range of clothes, including eveningwear and cocktail dresses, the Chanel Suit was the most popular.

The Chanel Suit was copied by Saks Fifth Avenue in the USA and Wallis, Jaeger and Marks & Spencer in London. Coco still took pleasure in imitation. With girlish glee, she told of a market trader selling fake Chanels: they went, she reported, like hot cakes. 'Come to my place and steal all the ideas you want,' she told the press. 'Fashion isn't made to be canned.'

In 1957 Dior died of a heart attack and his assistant, Yves Saint Laurent, took over. His first collection paid Chanel the complement of copying her. The next two – more **radically** his own – were less well received. She was sweetly cutting: 'Saint Laurent has excellent taste. The more he copies me, the better taste he displays.' Coco was again the undisputed leader of fashion.

Time, however, was moving on. In 1955, Adrienne, the only family member she cared about, died. (Chanel's brothers had died years before: Chanel made no effort to stay in touch with their children.) In

Coco Chanel selects fabrics in 1959. Despite projecting the image of a 'lady of leisure', Chanel was a tireless worker.

1960, Pierre Reverdy died in a Benedictine monastery at Solesmes, and in 1963 it was the turn of Jean Cocteau. Coco turned 80 in August 1963. She chose to forget her birthday.

In the 1960s, Chanel refined her classic look. She ridiculed other designers; calling Paco Rabanne, who used aluminium and plastics in his designs, 'the metallurgist'; criticizing Pierre Cardin for franchising his name and logo to every imaginable item – clothes, drinks, foods and perfumes.

By 1968, the Chanel empire was a multi-million pound per year business. Chanel had become a legend in her own lifetime: Coco – a musical based on her life, starring Katharine Hepburn – opened on Broadway. However, Chanel lived an increasingly lonely life. Surprisingly, when asked, she advised women to follow convention and marry. 'Otherwise she will need courage… and at the end she pays the terrible price of loneliness… Solitude can help a man find himself: it destroys a woman.' Men she loved never understood her work: 'The House of Chanel. It was my child. I made it, out of nothing.'

Chanel hated Sundays – a day empty of work. She had her chauffeur take her to Père Lachaise cemetery where she wandered among the tombs, talking to the dead, as she had done as a child. At home in the Ritz, she began sleepwalking, roaming the hotel corridors. Disgusted with herself, she ordered her personal staff to lock her in at night.

In 1970, Chanel suffered a slight stroke that paralyzed her right arm. She awoke to find a Catholic priest preparing the last rites. 'Too soon!' she hissed. After intense physiotherapy, Coco returned to work.

On the evening of Sunday 10 January 1971, Coco complained to her maid, Céline, that she could not breathe. Céline called the doctor but Chanel died before he arrived. Her final words were: 'You see, this is how you die.'

> " *'How many cares one loses when one decides not to be something but to be someone.'* Coco Chanel "

Though Chanel's life and opinions give us clues, her deliberate effort to hide the truth obscures her true character. She was human, with the faults and frailties of a human being. She could be cruel and crude about people – even **couturiers** who admired her. But she was also in the public eye and everything she said or did was noted or reacted to.

There are many contradictions in her life. Although given to strong outbursts – especially on the subject of the Wertheimers – her later relationship with Pierre Wertheimer was both cordial and professional. Chanel has also been accused of homophobia. However, while vulgarly uncomplimentary about the post-war designers – many of whom were gay – her friendship and support for gay men such as Cocteau is well known.

The legacy of Chanel

Cecil Beaton wrote, *'Chanel had… Talents that are very rare, she was a genius, and all her faults must be forgiven for that reason.'*

In 2000, *Time* magazine identified Coco Chanel as one of 100 people who made the 20th century. *Women.com* named her as one of their 100 women of the Millennium. Today, the House of Chanel is a **multinational** fashion and perfumes empire. In 1983, the

Coco Chanel, photographed by Horst P. Horst in 1937. This classic portrait established Horst's reputation as a photographer, and he would always be grateful to Chanel.

designer Karl Lagerfeld produced his first collection for the House of Chanel and now incorporates many of Coco Chanel's classic innovations into his own designs. Though very secretive about their finances, it has been estimated that the annual turnover of the Chanel group is in excess of US$2 billion (£1.2 billion)!

Ultimately, however, Coco Chanel will be remembered as an artist, an **iconoclast**, a revolutionary, and although she would have denied it, as a feminist. 'I was the one who changed, it wasn't fashion. I was the one who was in fashion.'

As Jean Cocteau observed, she brought to fashion the eye and techniques of the artist. As an iconoclast she ridiculed **belle époque** fashions and realized women's changing roles demanded new styles. After World War I, women's status would never be the same – and Chanel was ready with clothes that suited their growing independence. As the first 'star designer', she broke through rigid class barriers and joined a world of wealth and privilege. 'One did not talk to trades-people when I started. One did not recognize them if one ran into them at the races and one certainly didn't invite them to dinner.'

Chanel not only revolutionized fashion itself, but also the business of fashion, and had a major influence on generations of designers. She was at the centre of a **revolution** in art and culture, an intimate friend of the leading lights of the **avant-garde** and witness to and participant in some of the most notable artistic events of the 20th century.

Finally, though she denied she was a feminist, Coco Chanel lived as a feminist – succeeding as a businesswoman at a time when few women had such opportunities or had such an impact. She lived by her own rules and would not be intimidated into compromising them by others. She designed clothes that embodied the new, assertive, liberated woman. And she lived her life as the embodiment of the assertive, liberated woman.

> " Artist, writer and film-maker Jean Cocteau said, 'Chanel has, by a kind of miracle, worked in fashion according to rules that would seem to have value only for painters, musicians, poets.' "

Timeline

1883	Born 19 August, in the **hospice** in Saumur, in France.
1895	Mother, Jeanne, dies. Chanel and her two sisters are sent to the convent orphanage at Aubazine.
1900–02	Chanel and her sister Julia attend boarding school at Moulins.
1900–04	Works as a dressmaker with her aunt, Adrienne. Performs as a singer in Moulins and earns the nickname 'Coco'. Meets Etienne Balsan.
1905	Moves to Royallieu and lives there with Etienne Balsan.
1908	Meets Arthur 'Boy' Capel while holidaying with Balsan in the French Pyrénées.
1909	Opens her first **millinery** business in boulevard Malesherbes, Paris.
1910	With the support of Boy Capel, opens her boutique at 21 rue Cambon, Paris.
1912	The actress Gabrielle Dorziat is photographed wearing a range of Chanel hats.
1913	Encouraged by Boy, Chanel opens a fashion shop in the chic Normandy resort of Deauville. Sister Julia dies.
1914	Outbreak of World War I.
1915	Opens a *maison de couture* in Biarritz.
1916	Pioneers the use of jersey material as a fashion fabric.
1918	World War I ends.
1919	Acclaimed alongside the leading lights of the **avant-garde**. Boy Capel killed in road accident.
1920	Has an affair with Russian Grand Duke Dimitri in Biarritz. Introduces the first 'Chanel Suit' and cloche hat (1920s).
1921	Launches Chanel No.5 – and designs pioneering minimalist bottle. Opens a couture house at 31 rue Cambon, Paris.
1922	Designs costumes for Jean Cocteau's adaptation of *Antigone*. *Roubachka* – embroidered Russian peasant blouse is introduced.

1923 To increase the sales of Chanel No.5, signs a manufacturing and distribution agreement with the owners of Les Parfums Bourjois, Pierre and Paul Wertheimer.
First meets the Duke of Westminster.

1924 Creates Les Parfums Chanel in partnership with the Wertheimers.
Designs costumes for *Le Train Bleu*.
Begins relationship with Duke of Westminster.
Starts to design and popularize costume jewellery.

1926 Launches the groundbreaking 'little black dress'.

1929 The effects of the Wall Street Crash and the **Great Depression** hit the French fashion industry.

1930s Designs and refines a range of evening gowns and suits.
Continues to design costumes for stage, screen and ballet.

1931 Contracted by MGM to work in Hollywood, where she designs costumes for *Tonight or Never*.
Begins relationship with Paul Iribe.

1932 Returns to Paris and is commissioned to design a range of diamond jewellery.

1934 Announces intended marriage to Paul Iribe; he dies of a heart attack before they can marry.

1939 At the declaration of World War II, closes her *haute couture* salons.

1940 First flees then returns to Paris. Settles back in the Hotel Ritz.
Meets Hans Gunther von Dincklage – 'Spatz' – and they begin a relationship.

1943 Plans to meet Winston Churchill in what becomes known as Operation *Modellhut*.

1945 World War II ends.
Leaves for Lausanne, Switzerland.

1954 Chanel's comeback aged 71: the range included suits, overcoats, cocktail dresses, eveningwear and costume jewellery.

1968 Coco, a Broadway musical based on Chanel's life, opens in New York.

1971 Dies at the Hotel Ritz, Paris, on 10 January, aged 87.

Glossary

abortion surgical termination of a pregnancy

affluent society name given to the relatively wealthy post-war world of the 1950s

Allies refers to those countries in alliance against Germany in World War II. These included the UK, the Soviet Union, France, Australia and the USA.

androgynous having both male and female characteristics and therefore being of indeterminate sex

anti-Semitism anti-Jewish feelings and actions

avant-garde pioneers or innovators in any sphere of the arts

belle époque the fine period before World War I

blackout turning off all visible lights to hinder aerial bombing missions

Bolshevism describes the violent, revolutionary communism alive in Russia at the time

Claudines new breed of feminine heroines inspired by the works of the novelist Colette

collaborator someone who assists or cooperates with invaders

conscript to call up into the army

couturier person who designs, makes or sells fashionable clothes

depression period of serious economic crisis, featuring high unemployment and rising numbers of company closures

detoxification cure undertaken by alcoholics and drug-addicts to clear their bodies of toxic drugs

dowry money that a woman brings into a marriage: the greater the dowry, the more attractive a proposition a woman becomes

Eastern Front most advanced easterly position of battle, and the scene of conflict between the German and Russian armies

elite the rich upper classes, a superior or select few

elitist person who believes in a natural hierarchy of rulers and ruled

etiquette social manners and rules of correct behaviour

exiles individuals persecuted and driven from their country of origin

Fascist member of Fascist party which ruled in Italy from 1922–43, characterized by extreme militarism and anti-communism

fertility ability to get pregnant and have children

franchise permission given by a company for a retailer to sell its goods

Free French French government-in-exile led by Charles de Gaulle during World War II

garrison town town where lots of soldiers are based

Great Depression economic slump that followed the Wall Street Stock Market crash of 1929. Businesses failed and unemployment rose dramatically.

haute couture high-class dressmaking

hospice hostel for homeless or poverty stricken families and individuals; often supported by church funds, charities or town councils

'hourglass' exaggerated feminine shape, resembling the shape of an hourglass, achieved by using tight corsets

iconoclast person who attacks the beliefs that many people hold dear

illegitimate being born to parents who are not married

illiterate unable to read and write

industrialization growth of industry, mass production and the factory system

inferiority complex a suppressed sense that a person is lower in worth to others with whom they mix

Jazz Age period of wealth, freedom and hedonism between the end of World War I and the beginning of the Great Depression in 1929: sometimes called the Roaring Twenties

maisons de couture companies ('houses') of fashion and design

mannequin person who models clothing

mass market large-scale consumer market for products, and the development of manufacturing techniques capable of satisfying it

mass production industrial production based on the factory and the production line to cater for the mass market

milliner hat-maker

Modernism name given to the art movement of the early 20th century, characterized by the use of unusual and unconventional subject matter

multinational very large company that is not based in a single country but is divided between several countries, and has a worldwide market for the goods it produces

nationalist putting the interest of one nation and national group above all else, and turning against outsiders, foreigners, foreign powers and religious minorities

New York Stock Exchange centre for the buying and selling of shares in companies, on Wall Street, USA

pagan fertility rite ceremony associated with pre-Christian religion, to make the land fertile for crops

parasol umbrella that protects people from the sun

paternalistic limiting people's freedom in the same way that a father controls his children

picket line line of strikers outside a workplace during an industrial dispute

Popular Front alliance of communists and socialists that contested and won the 1936 elections in France

power of attorney delegated authority: legal permission to act on another's behalf

propaganda biased broadcasts and news-stories

radical term describing intense and far-reaching political, social, cultural and/or artistic change

rayon a silk-like synthetic fibre

ready-to-wear ready-made fashions bought off the peg

republican person who believes in a system of government with an elected head of state and without a royal family

resistance organized opposition to invaders

revolution extreme and rapid change brought about by single-minded, violent or confrontational means

right-wing having conservative political views, being opposed to socialism

royalty payment made to a designer, author and so on for copies of their work sold

Russian Revolution takeover of power in Russia in 1917 by the Communists lead by Vladimir Lenin, which ended the rule of the Russian royal family

satire comedy that pokes fun at popular beliefs or opinions

semi-autobiographical fictionalized accounts based on the writer's own life

sit-down strike when workers come to their place of work but refuse to either work or go home

socialist person who believes in a more equal distribution of wealth and goods

stays rigid pieces of whalebone that kept women's corsets stiff to emphasize an idealized shape

suffrage right to vote in a society. Universal suffrage is the right of all citizens, regardless of sex, creed, religion, income or class to vote in elections.

surrealist person involved in the artistic movement called Surrealism, established by André Breton and others in the 1920s. Surrealists promoted the use of humour, details from dreams and absurd mixtures of words and pictures.

synthetic artificial, man-made

urbanization the increasing concentration of the population in large towns and cities, where they were employed in huge new factories

women's rights the assertion of equal rights for women: the right to vote, to work and for equal treatment before the law

Places of interest and further reading

Places to visit

Museums now take the history of fashion and costume very seriously and some will have displays that feature a small number of costumes and pieces of jewellery by Chanel. Permanent exhibitions can be found at:

The V&A Museum, Cromwell Road, South Kensington, London SW7 2RL, Tel: 020 7942 2000, www.vam.ac.uk – has lots of information and exhibitions on textiles and dress, with a number of Chanel pieces on display.

Larger displays on the history of fashion are often temporary rather than permanent, so it is worth taking note of any upcoming exhibitions in your locality.

Websites

There are many articles about Coco Chanel, the House of Chanel Corporation and the history of fashion on the Web. Why not try a name search on a search engine? Here are a few websites which you might like to visit:

www.britannica.com – features biographical information on Coco Chanel and links to other articles and features about her. It also has information about many of Chanel's famous friends and contemporaries.

www.chanel.com – the official website of the Chanel company. This website does not have anything on Coco Chanel herself, but has plenty of information about Chanel fashion today.

www.fashionwindows.com – a website with masses of information about the world of fashion, fashion designers and the history of fashion.

www.time.com/time/time100 – for information on the 100 most influential people in the 20th century.

Sources

Chanel The Couturiere At Work, Amy de la Haye, Shelley Tobin (The Victoria and Albert Museum, London 1994)

Coco Chanel, Alice Mackrell (BT Batsford, London 1992)

Coco Chanel, A Biography, Axel Madsen (Bloomsbury, London 1990)

Chanel and her World, Edmonde Charles Roux (Weidenfield and Nicholson, London 1981)

There are also many books on the history of fashion that put Coco Chanel in context. These include:

History of 20th-Century Fashion, Elizabeth Ewing (BT Batsford, London 1992)

The History of Haute Couture 1850–1950, Diana de Marly (Batsford, London 1980)

Vogue History of 20th-Century Fashion, Jane Mulvagh (Viking, London 1988)

Further reading

In addition to the above, the following may also be useful:

Coco Chanel. Her Life, Her Secrets, Marcel Haedrich (Little, Brown and Co., New York 1971)

Twentieth Century World, Living through History series, Nigel Kelly, Rosemary Rees and Jane Shuter (Heinemann Library, Oxford 1988)

Trends in Textile Technology series, Hazel King (Heinemann Library, Oxford 2000)

20th Century Fashion series, various authors (Heinemann Library, Oxford 1999)

Index